More Christmas Piano Solos

For All Piano Methods

Table of Contents

	Page No.	CD Track

Book: ISBN 978-1-4234-8363-2
Book/CD: ISBN 978-1-4234-9328-0

HAL•LEONARD®
CORPORATION
7777 W. BLUEMOUND RD. P.O. BOX 13819 MILWAUKEE, WI 53213

Visit Hal Leonard Online at
www.halleonard.com

Angels from the Realms of Glory

Words by James Montgomery
Music by Henry T. Smart
Arranged by Jennifer Linn

Joyfully (♩ = 108) 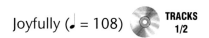 **TRACKS 1/2**

Play both hands one octave higher throughout.

An - gels from the realms of glo - ry,
Sa - ges, leave your con - tem - pla - tions,

mp a tempo

wing your flight o'er all the earth.
bright - er vi - sions gleam a - far.

Ye who sang cre -
Seek the great de -

a - tion's sto - ry, now pro - claim Mes - si - ah's birth.

sire of na - tions; ye have seen His ___ na - tal star.

mf

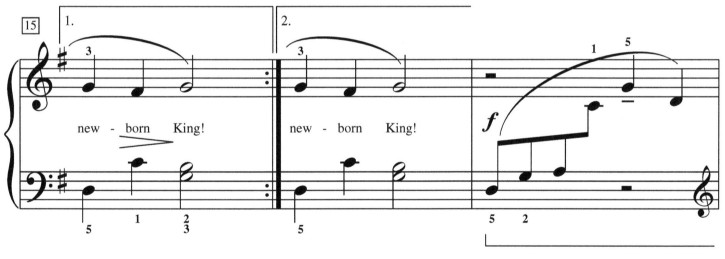

Come and wor - ship! Come and wor - ship! Wor - ship Christ, the

f

1. new - born King!

2. new - born King!

f

18

rit.

p

White Christmas

from the Motion Picture Irving Berlin's HOLIDAY INN

Words and Music by Irving Berlin
Arranged by Mona Rejino

Accompaniment (Student plays one octave higher than written.)

TRACKS 3/4

Moderately, with expression (♩ = 108)

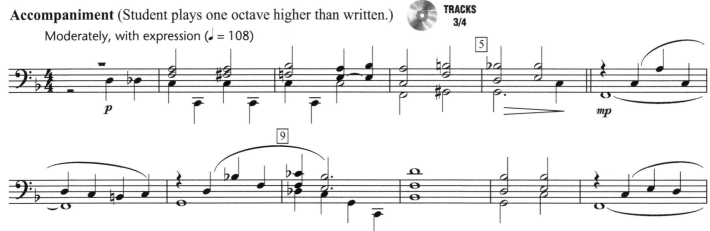

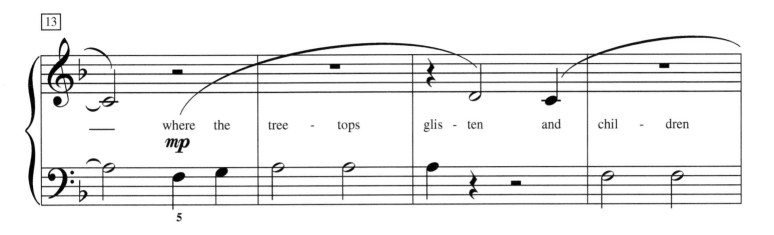

where the tree-tops glis-ten and chil-dren

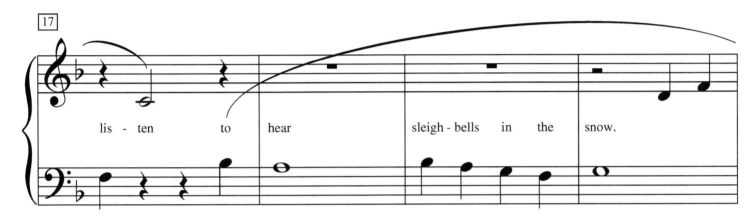

lis-ten to hear sleigh-bells in the snow.

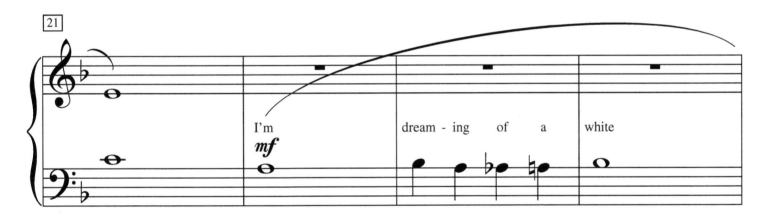

I'm dream-ing of a white

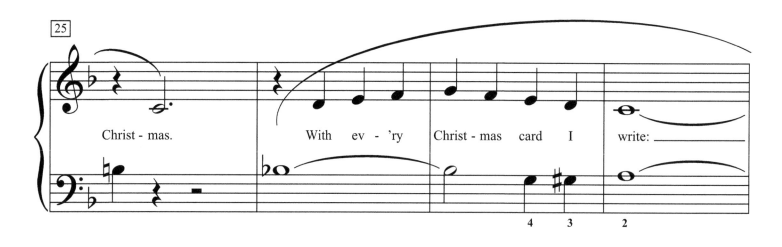

Christ - mas.   With ev - 'ry Christ - mas card I write: ____

4   3   2

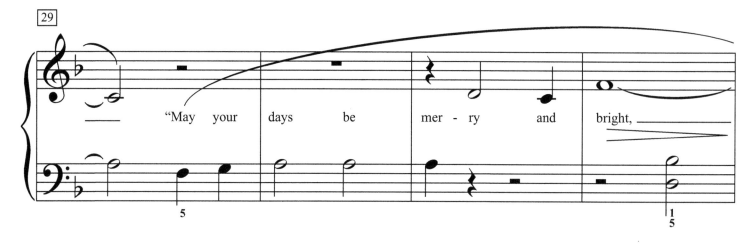

____ "May your days be mer - ry and bright, ____

5   1
                                                         5

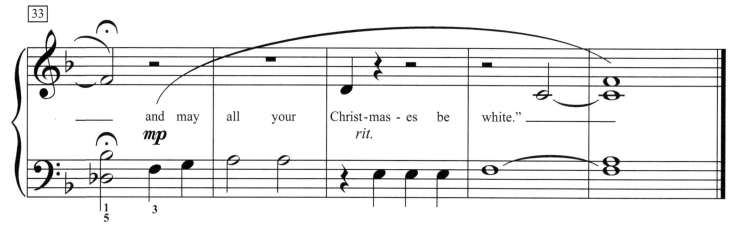

____ and may all your Christ-mas - es be white." ____

mp   *rit.*

1
5   3

p

rit.

Christmas Time Is Here

from A CHARLIE BROWN CHRISTMAS

Words by Lee Mendelson
Music by Vince Guaraldi
Arranged by Phillip Keveren

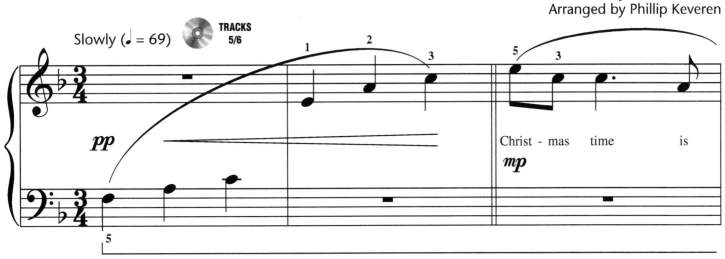

year. Snow-flakes in the air,

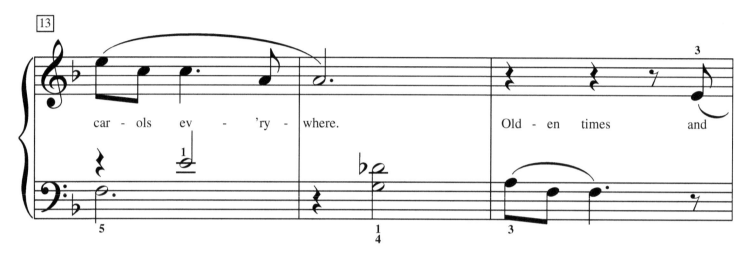

car - ols ev - 'ry - where. Old - en times and

an - cient rhymes of love and dreams to share.

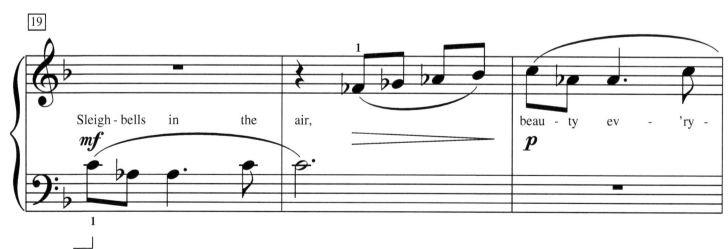

Sleigh-bells in the air, beau - ty ev - 'ry -

mf *p*

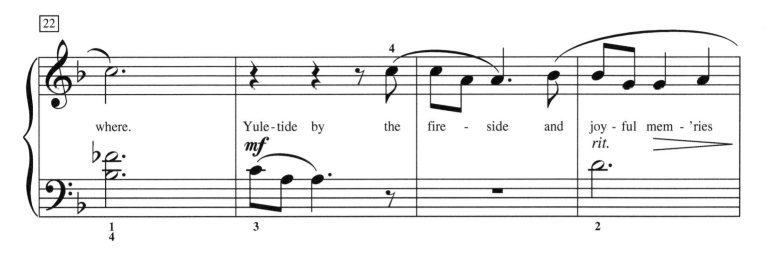

where. Yule-tide by the fire - side and joy - ful mem - 'ries

mf　　*rit.*

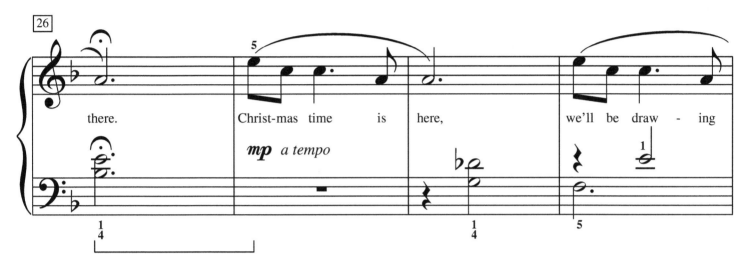

there. Christ-mas time is here, we'll be draw - ing

mp *a tempo*

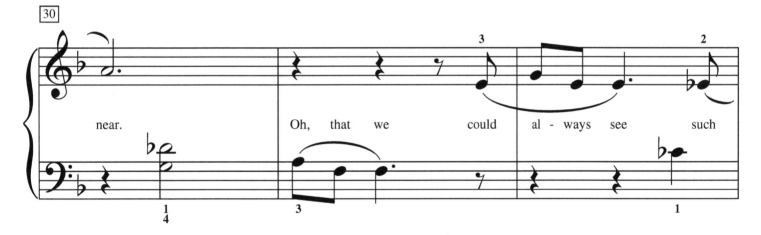

near. Oh, that we could al - ways see such

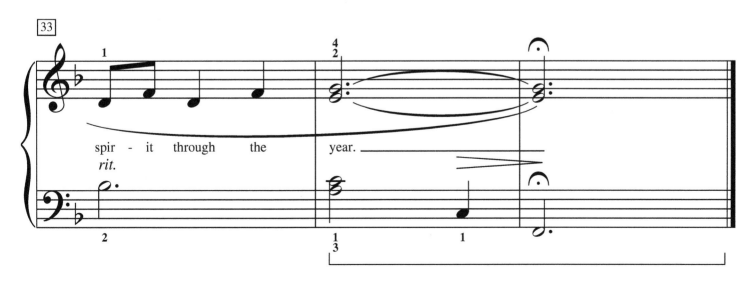

spir - it through the year. _____

rit.

Jingle Bells

Words and Music by
J. Pierpont
Arranged by Carol Klose

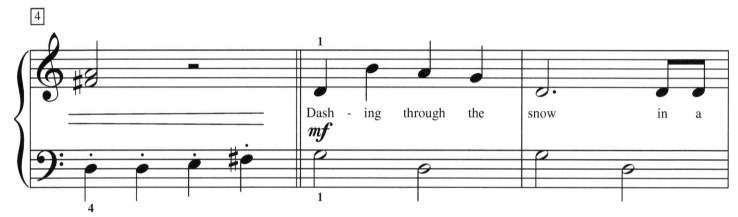

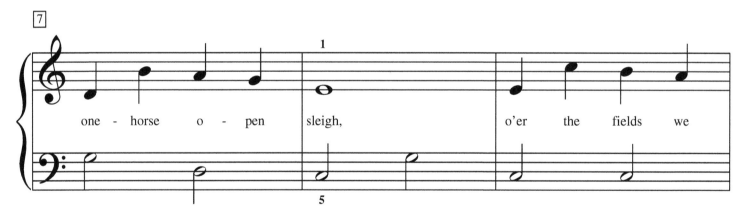

Accompaniment (Student plays one octave higher than written.) **TRACKS 7/8**

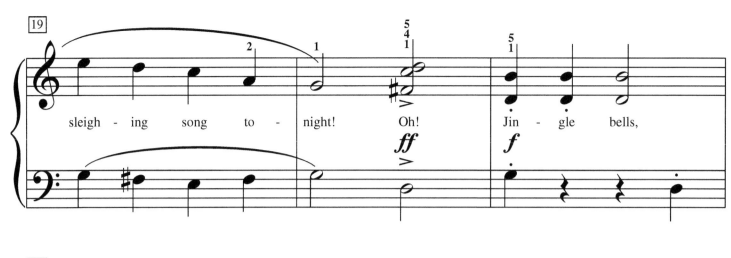

sleigh - ing song to - night! Oh! Jin - gle bells,

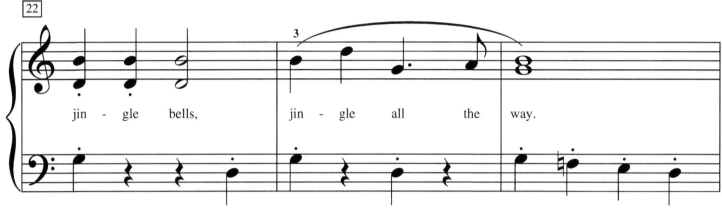

jin - gle bells, jin - gle all the way.

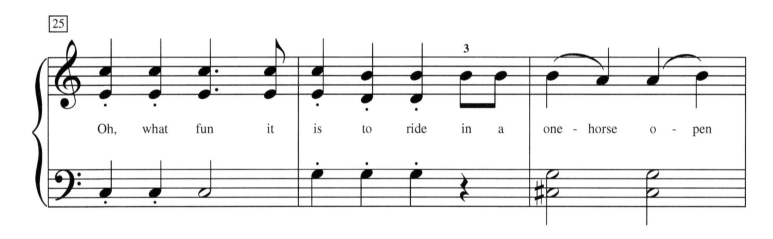

Oh, what fun it is to ride in a one - horse o - pen

Once in Royal David's City

Words by Cecil F. Alexander
Music by Henry J. Gauntlett
Arranged by Phillip Keveren

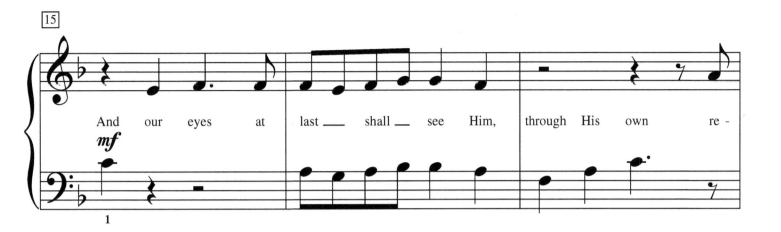

And our eyes at last shall see Him, through His own re-

deem - ing love. For That Child so dear and gen - tle is our Lord in

heav'n a - bove; and He leads His chil - dren on to the place where

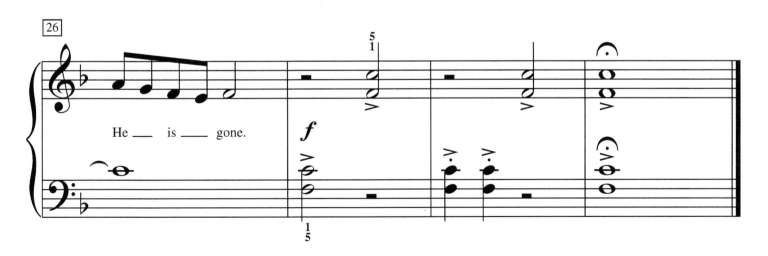

He is gone.

Here We Come A-Wassailing

Traditional
Arranged by Fred Kern

joy come to you, and to you your was - sail

too; And God bless you and send _____ you a

mf

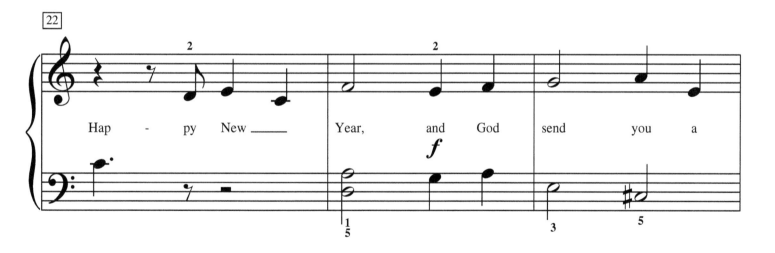

Hap - py New _____ Year, and God send you a

f

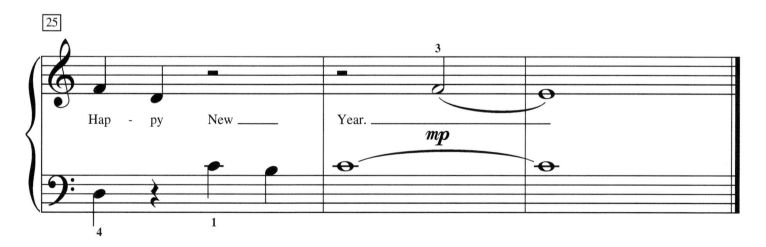

Hap - py New _____ Year. _____

mp

Suzy Snowflake

Words and Music by Sid Tepper
and Roy Bennett
Arranged by Fred Kern

Here comes Su - zy Snow - flake, dressed in a snow white

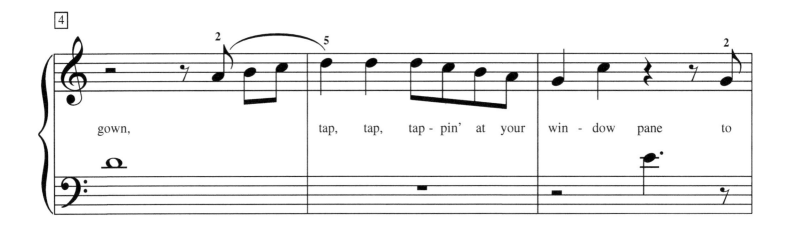

gown, tap, tap, tap - pin' at your win - dow pane to

Accompaniment (Student plays one octave higher than written.) TRACKS 13/14

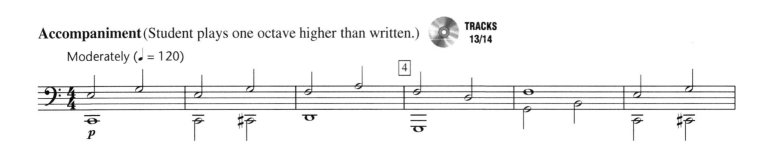

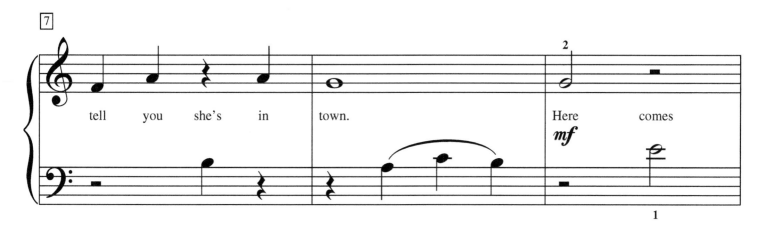

tell you she's in town. Here comes

Su - zy Snow - flake, soon you will hear her say:

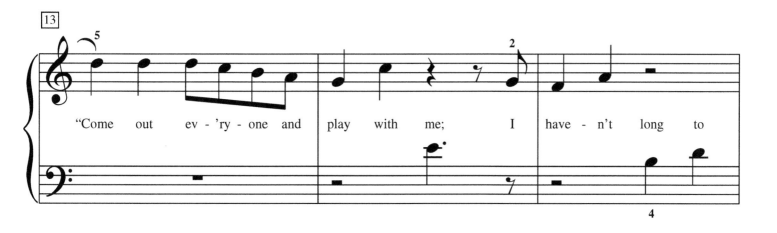

"Come out ev - 'ry - one and play with me; I have - n't long to

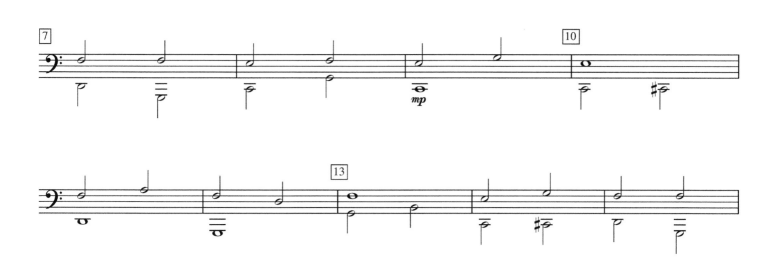

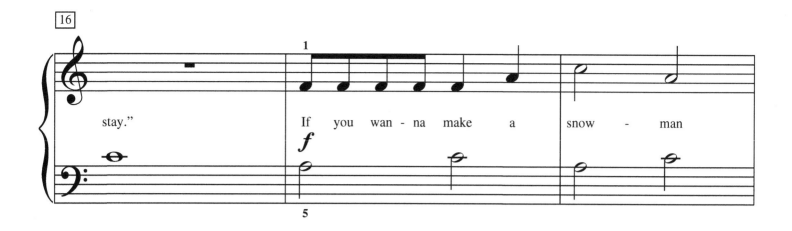

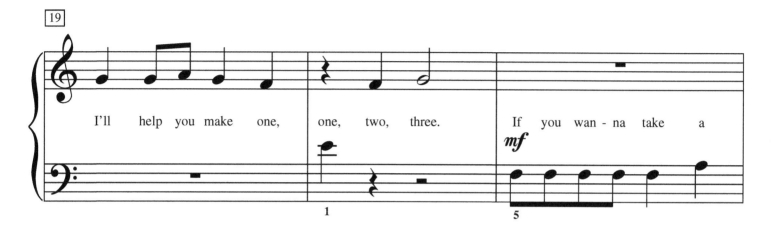

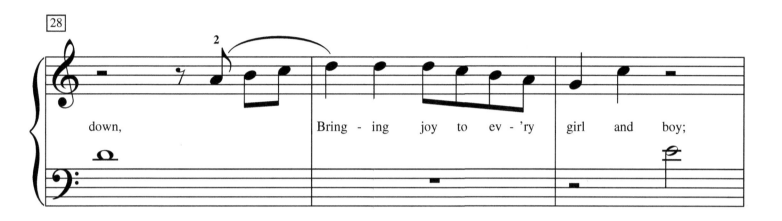

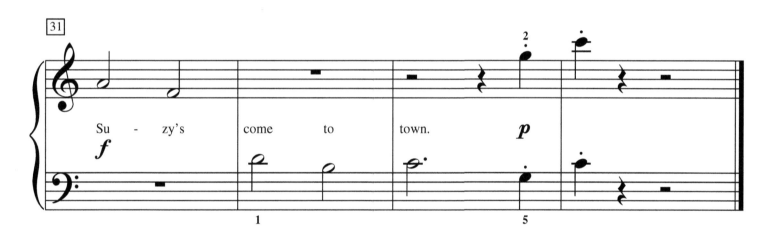

Blue Christmas

Words and Music by Billy Hayes
and Jay Johnson
Arranged by Phillip Keveren

ra - tions of red on a green Christ - mas

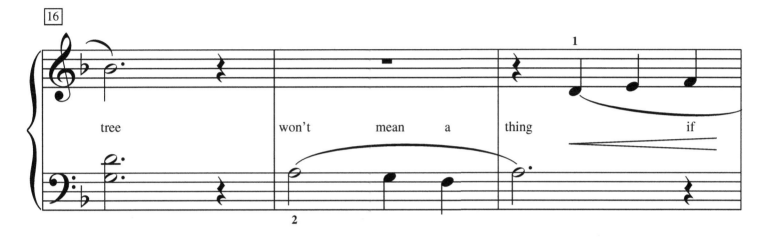

tree won't mean a thing if

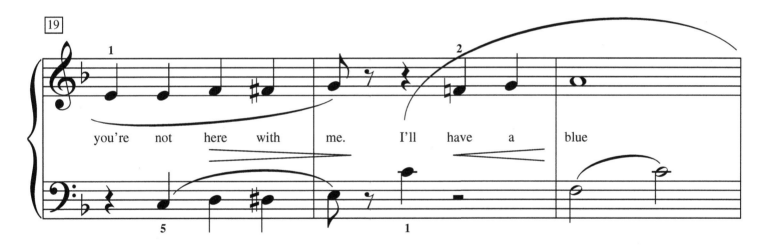

you're not here with me. I'll have a blue

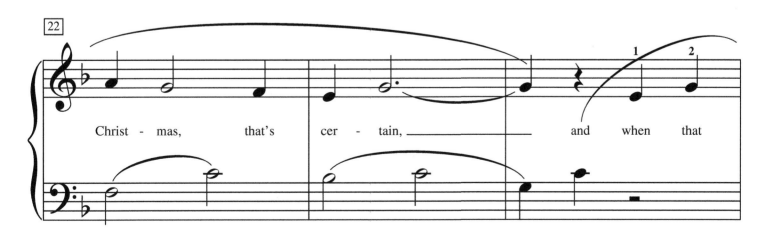

Christ - mas, that's cer - tain, _____ and when that

23

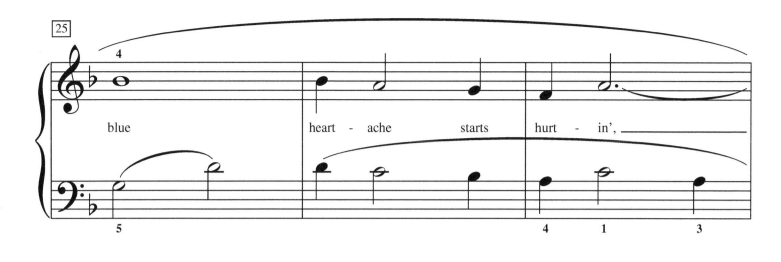

blue   heart - ache   starts   hurt - in', _____

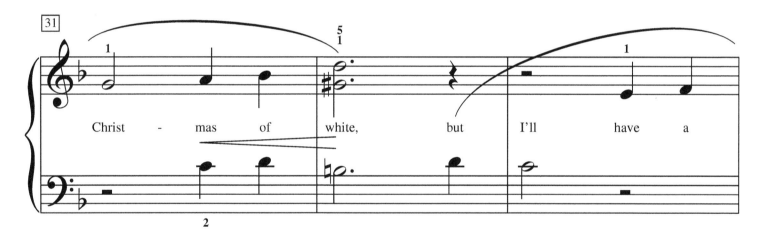

_____ you'll be   do - in' al - right   with   your

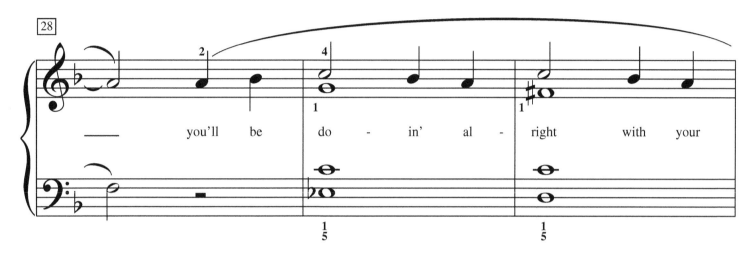

Christ - mas   of   white,   but   I'll   have   a

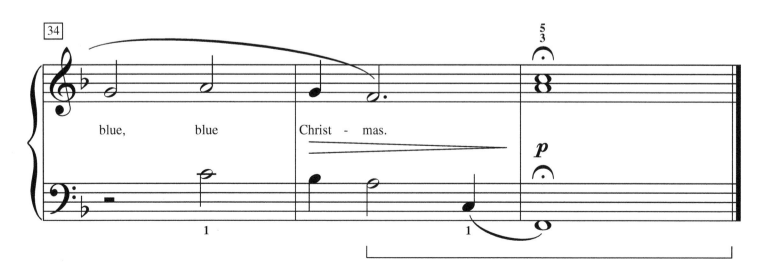

blue,   blue   Christ - mas.

I Saw Mommy Kissing Santa Claus

Words and Music by
Tommie Connor
Arranged by Mona Rejino

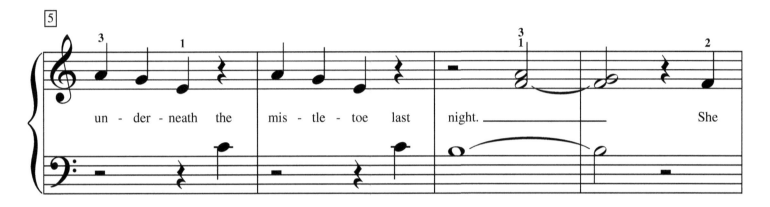

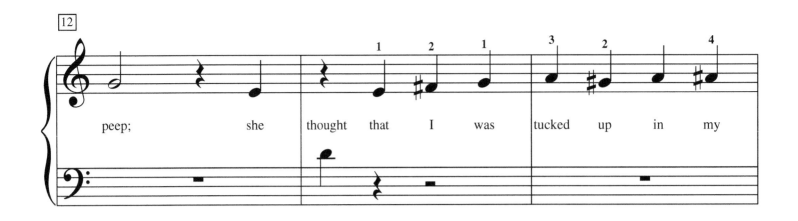

peep; she thought that I was tucked up in my

bed - room fast a - sleep. Then I saw

Mom - my tick - le San - ta Claus, un - der - neath his

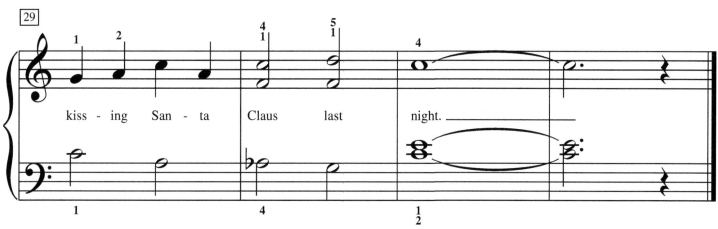

Coventry Carol

Words by Robert Croo
Traditional English Melody
Arranged by Mona Rejino

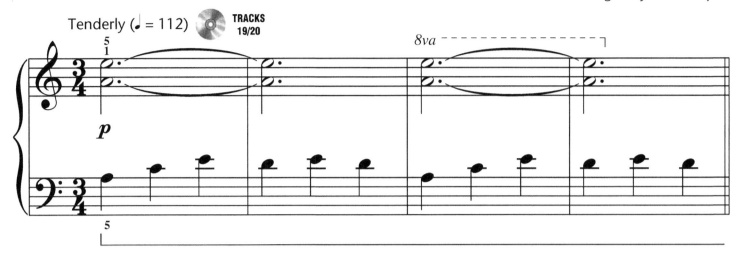

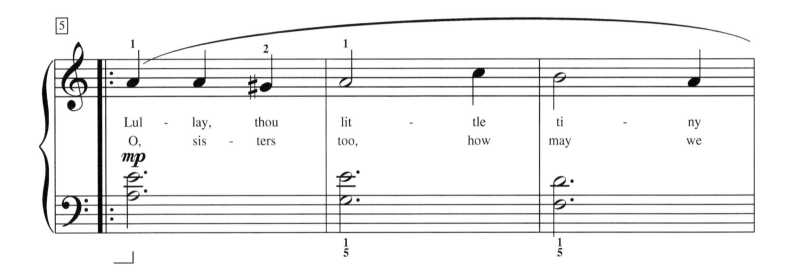

Lul - lay,   thou   lit - tle   ti - ny
O,   sis - ters too,   how   may   we

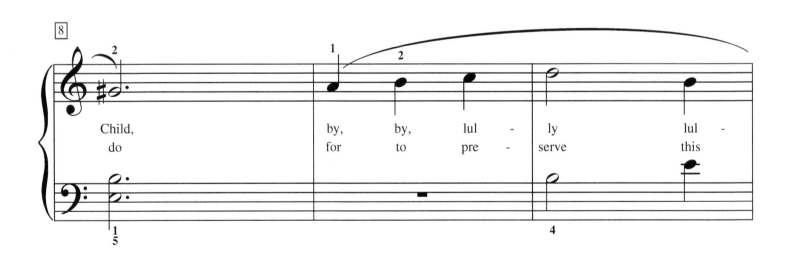

Child,   by,   by,   lul - ly   lul -
do   for   to   pre - serve   this

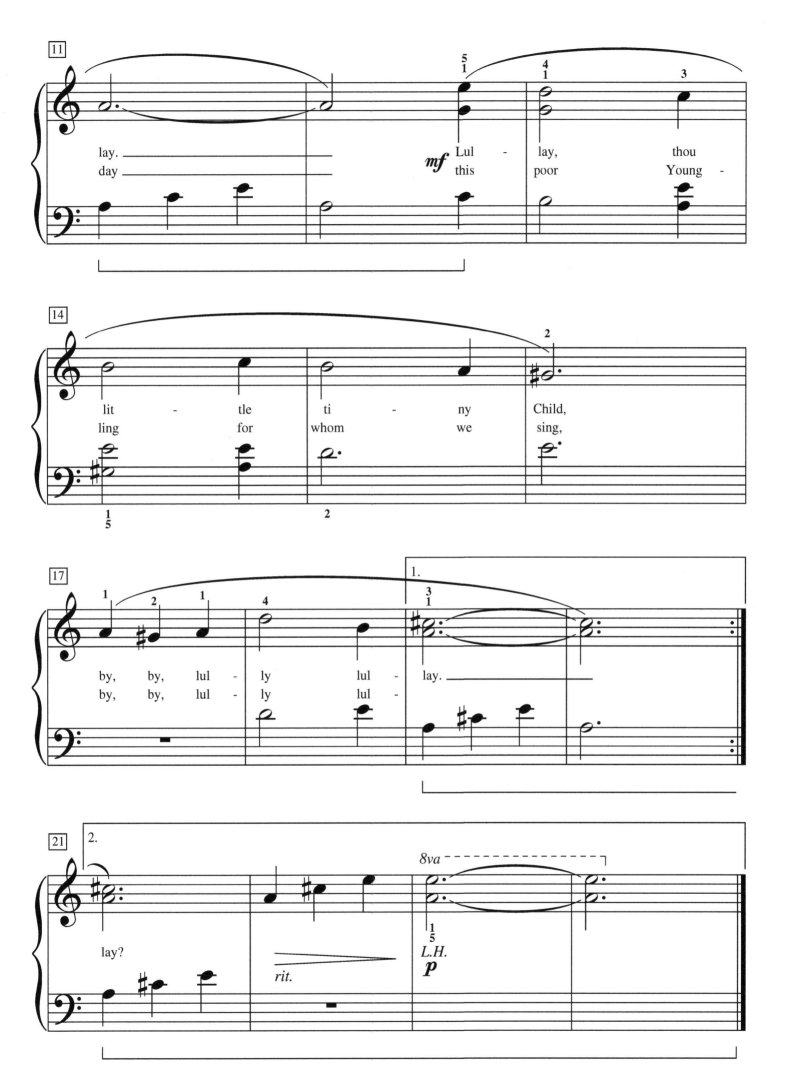

Pat-A-Pan

Secondo

Music by Bernard de la Monnoye
Arranged by Carol Klose

Medium March tempo (♩ = 104-120) TRACKS 21/22
Both hands play one octave lower than written throughout.

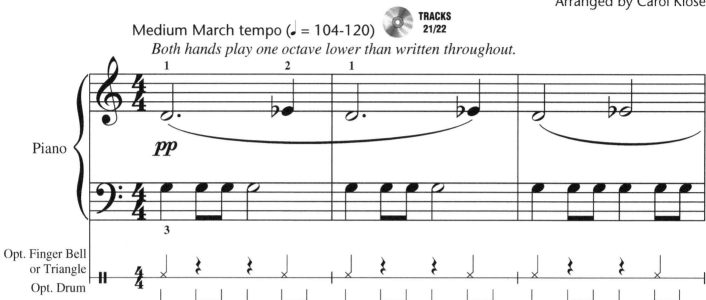

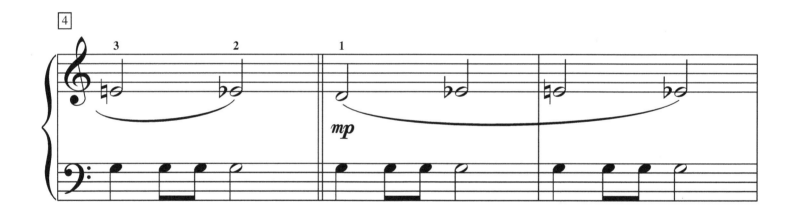

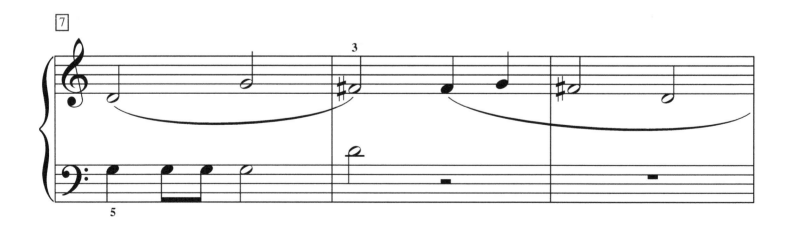

Pat-A-Pan

Primo

Music by Bernard de la Monnoye
Arranged by Carol Klose

Medium March tempo (♩ = 104-120) **TRACKS 23/24**

Both hands play one octave higher than written throughout.

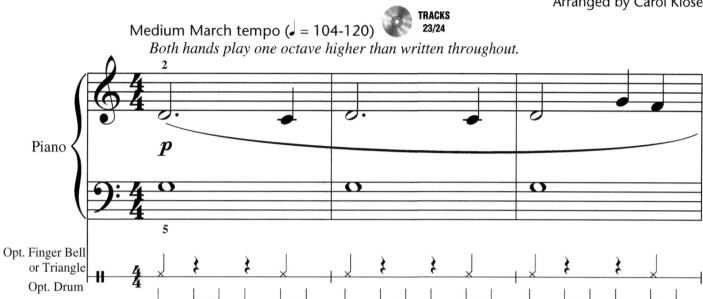

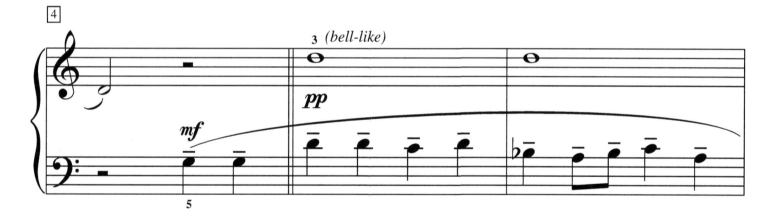

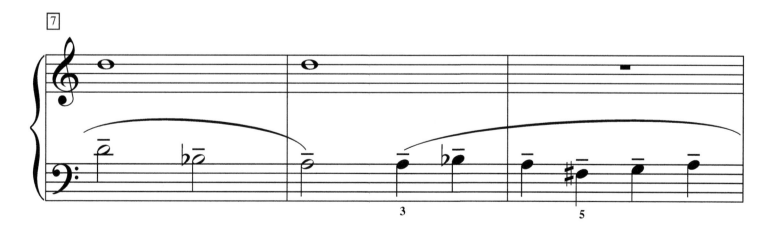

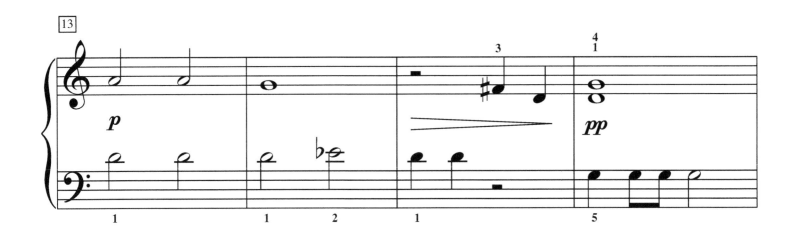

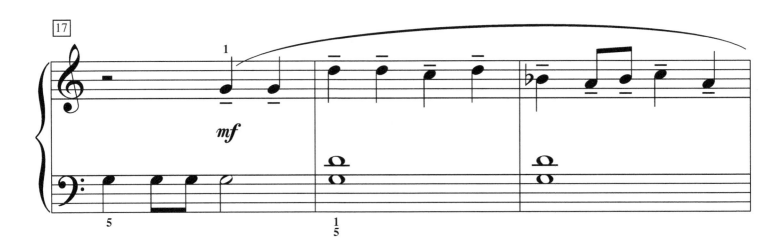

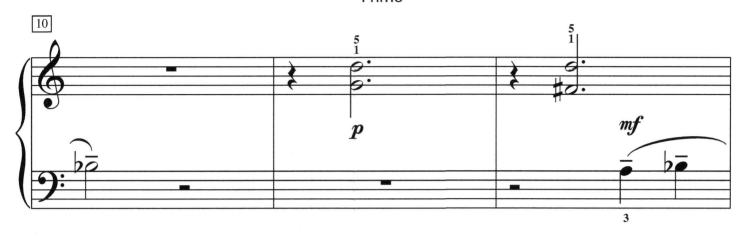

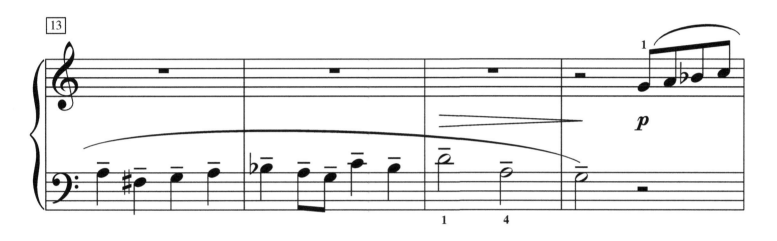

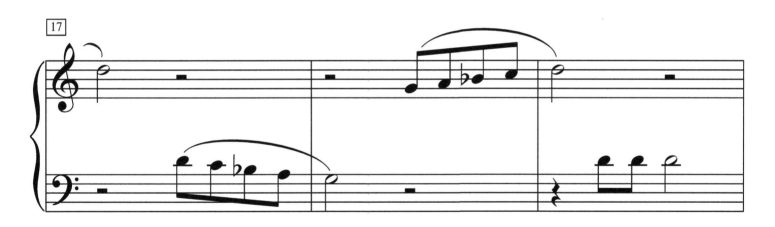

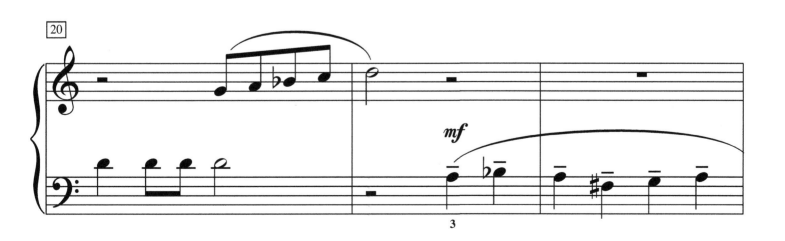

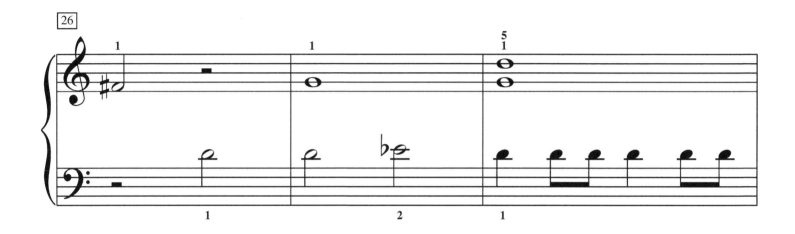

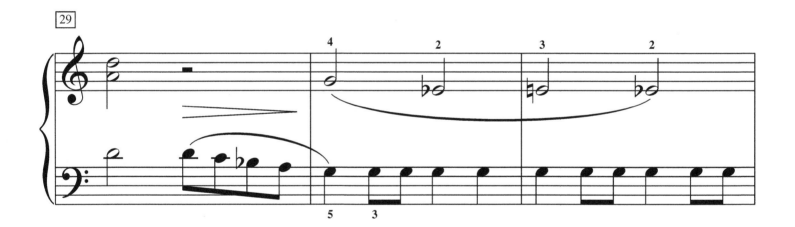

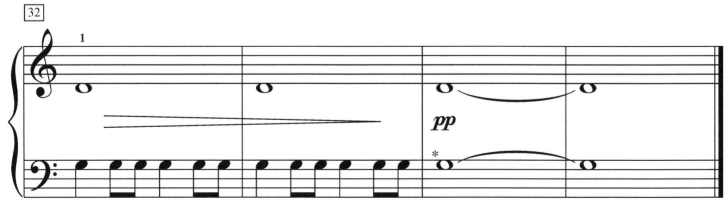

Opt. drum accompaniment ends here.

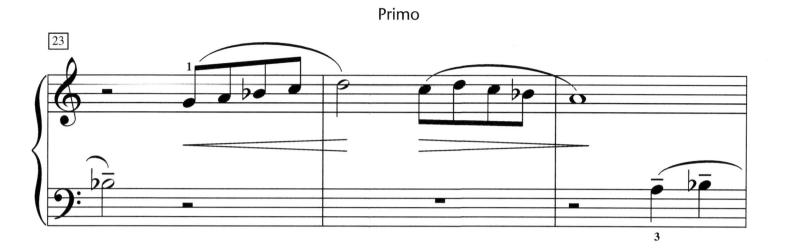

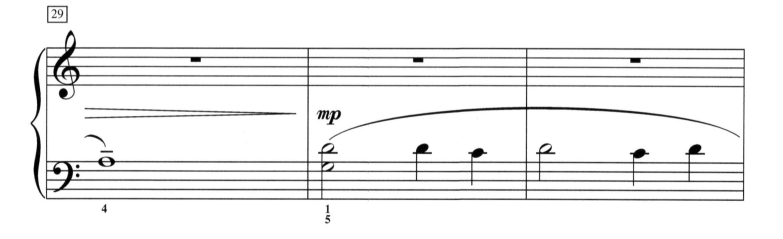

Opt. drum accompaniment ends here.

Silver and Gold

Music and Lyrics by
Johnny Marks
Arranged by Carol Klose

Sil - ver and gold,

sil - ver and gold, ev - 'ry - one

wish - es for sil - ver and gold.

COMPOSER SHOWCASE
HAL LEONARD STUDENT PIANO LIBRARY

This series showcases great original piano music from our **Hal Leonard Student Piano Library** family of composers. Carefully graded for easy selection.

BILL BOYD

JAZZ BITS (AND PIECES)
Early Intermediate Level
00290312 11 Solos......................$7.99

JAZZ DELIGHTS
Intermediate Level
00240435 11 Solos......................$8.99

JAZZ FEST
Intermediate Level
00240436 10 Solos......................$8.99

JAZZ PRELIMS
Early Elementary Level
00290032 12 Solos......................$7.99

JAZZ SKETCHES
Intermediate Level
00220001 8 Solos......................$8.99

JAZZ STARTERS
Elementary Level
00290425 10 Solos......................$8.99

JAZZ STARTERS II
Late Elementary Level
00290434 11 Solos......................$7.99

JAZZ STARTERS III
Late Elementary Level
00290465 12 Solos......................$8.99

THINK JAZZ!
Early Intermediate Level
00290417 Method Book............$12.99

TONY CARAMIA

JAZZ MOODS
Intermediate Level
00296728 8 Solos......................$6.95

SUITE DREAMS
Intermediate Level
00296775 4 Solos......................$6.99

SONDRA CLARK

DAKOTA DAYS
Intermediate Level
00296521 5 Solos......................$6.95

FLORIDA FANTASY SUITE
Intermediate Level
00296766 3 Duets......................$7.95

THREE ODD METERS
Intermediate Level
00296472 3 Duets......................$6.95

MATTHEW EDWARDS

CONCERTO FOR YOUNG PIANISTS
FOR 2 PIANOS, FOUR HANDS
Intermediate Level Book/CD
00296356 3 Movements $19.99

CONCERTO NO. 2 IN G MAJOR
FOR 2 PIANOS, 4 HANDS
Intermediate Level Book/CD
00296670 3 Movements............$17.99

PHILLIP KEVEREN

MOUSE ON A MIRROR
Late Elementary Level
00296361 5 Solos......................$8.99

MUSICAL MOODS
Elementary/Late Elementary Level
00296714 7 Solos......................$6.99

SHIFTY-EYED BLUES
Late Elementary Level
00296374 5 Solos......................$7.99

CAROL KLOSE

THE BEST OF CAROL KLOSE
Early to Late Intermediate Level
00146151 15 Solos..................$12.99

CORAL REEF SUITE
Late Elementary Level
00296354 7 Solos......................$7.50

DESERT SUITE
Intermediate Level
00296667 6 Solos......................$7.99

FANCIFUL WALTZES
Early Intermediate Level
00296473 5 Solos......................$7.95

GARDEN TREASURES
Late Intermediate Level
00296787 5 Solos......................$8.50

ROMANTIC EXPRESSIONS
Intermediate to Late Intermediate Level
00296923 5 Solos......................$8.99

WATERCOLOR MINIATURES
Early Intermediate Level
00296848 7 Solos......................$7.99

JENNIFER LINN

AMERICAN IMPRESSIONS
Intermediate Level
00296471 6 Solos......................$8.99

ANIMALS HAVE FEELINGS TOO
Early Elementary/Elementary Level
00147789 8 Solos......................$8.99

AU CHOCOLAT
Late Elementary/Early Intermediate Level
00298110 7 Solos......................$8.99

CHRISTMAS IMPRESSIONS
Intermediate Level
00296706 8 Solos......................$8.99

JUST PINK
Elementary Level
00296722 9 Solos......................$8.99

LES PETITES IMAGES
Late Elementary Level
00296664 7 Solos......................$8.99

LES PETITES IMPRESSIONS
Intermediate Level
00296355 6 Solos......................$8.99

REFLECTIONS
Late Intermediate Level
00296843 5 Solos......................$8.99

TALES OF MYSTERY
Intermediate Level
00296769 6 Solos......................$8.99

LYNDA LYBECK-ROBINSON

ALASKA SKETCHES
Early Intermediate Level
00119637 8 Solos......................$8.99

AN AWESOME ADVENTURE
Late Elementary Level
00137563 8 Solos......................$7.99

FOR THE BIRDS
Early Intermediate/Intermediate Level
00237078 9 Solos......................$8.99

WHISPERING WOODS
Late Elementary Level
00275905 9 Solos......................$8.99

MONA REJINO

CIRCUS SUITE
Late Elementary Level
00296665 5 Solos......................$8.99

COLOR WHEEL
Early Intermediate Level
00201951 6 Solos......................$9.99

IMPRESIONES DE ESPAÑA
Intermediate Level
00337520 6 Solos......................$8.99

IMPRESSIONS OF NEW YORK
Intermediate Level
00364212......................$8.99

JUST FOR KIDS
Elementary Level
00296840 8 Solos......................$7.99

MERRY CHRISTMAS MEDLEYS
Intermediate Level
00296799 5 Solos......................$8.99

MINIATURES IN STYLE
Intermediate Level
00148088 6 Solos......................$8.99

PORTRAITS IN STYLE
Early Intermediate Level
00296507 6 Solos......................$8.99

EUGÉNIE ROCHEROLLE

CELEBRATION SUITE
Intermediate Level
00152724 3 Duets......................$8.99

ENCANTOS ESPAÑOLES (SPANISH DELIGHTS)
Intermediate Level
00125451 6 Solos......................$8.99

JAMBALAYA
Intermediate Level
00296654 2 Pianos, 8 Hands.....$12.99
00296725 2 Pianos, 4 Hands.......$7.95

JEROME KERN CLASSICS
Intermediate Level
00296577 10 Solos....................$12.99

LITTLE BLUES CONCERTO
Early Intermediate Level
00142801 2 Pianos, 4 Hands......$12.99

TOUR FOR TWO
Late Elementary Level
00296832 6 Duets......................$9.99

TREASURES
Late Elementary/Early Intermediate Level
00296924 7 Solos......................$8.99

JEREMY SISKIND

BIG APPLE JAZZ
Intermediate Level
00278209 8 Solos......................$8.99

MYTHS AND MONSTERS
Late Elementary/Early Intermediate Level
00148148 9 Solos......................$8.99

CHRISTOS TSITSAROS

DANCES FROM AROUND THE WORLD
Early Intermediate Level
00296688 7 Solos......................$8.99

FIVE SUMMER PIECES
Late Intermediate/Advanced Level
00361235 5 Solos......................$12.99

LYRIC BALLADS
Intermediate/Late Intermediate Level
00102404 6 Solos......................$8.99

POETIC MOMENTS
Intermediate Level
00296403 8 Solos......................$8.99

SEA DIARY
Early Intermediate Level
00253486 9 Solos......................$8.99

SONATINA HUMORESQUE
Late Intermediate Level
00296772 3 Movements..............$6.99

SONGS WITHOUT WORDS
Intermediate Level
00296506 9 Solos......................$9.99

THREE PRELUDES
Early Advanced Level
00130747 3 Solos......................$8.99

THROUGHOUT THE YEAR
Late Elementary Level
00296723 12 Duets....................$6.95

ADDITIONAL COLLECTIONS

AT THE LAKE
by Elvina Pearce
Elementary/Late Elementary Level
00131642 10 Solos and Duets.....$7.99

CHRISTMAS FOR TWO
by Dan Fox
Early Intermediate Level
00290069 13 Duets....................$8.99

CHRISTMAS JAZZ
by Mike Springer
Intermediate Level
00296525 6 Solos......................$8.99

COUNTY RAGTIME FESTIVAL
by Fred Kern
Intermediate Level
00296882 7 Solos......................$7.99

LITTLE JAZZERS
by Jennifer Watts
Elementary/Late Elementary Level
00154573 9 Solos......................$8.99

PLAY THE BLUES!
by Luann Carman
Early Intermediate Level
00296357 10 Solos....................$9.99

ROLLER COASTERS & RIDES
by Jennifer & Mike Watts
Intermediate Level
00131144 8 Duets......................$8.99

Prices, contents, and availability subject to change without notice.